Monster Trucks

Quinn M. Arnold

seedlings

CREATIVE EDUCATION • CREATIVE PAPERBACKS

Published by Creative Education and Creative Paperbacks
P.O. Box 227, Mankato, Minnesota 56002
Creative Education and Creative Paperbacks
are imprints of The Creative Company
www.thecreativecompany.us

Design by Ellen Huber; production by Joe Kahnke
Art direction by Rita Marshall
Printed in the United States of America

Photographs by Alamy (Ian Dagnall, Michael Doolittle, PCN
Photography), Dreamstime (Alterfalter, Serena Livingston,
Natursports, Kutt Niinepuu, Njnightsky, Brian Sullivan, Jenta
Wong, Michal Zacharzewski), Flickr (Ben Beard, Kiri Leach,
Mike, Seluryar), Shutterstock (EvrenKalinbacak, Steve Lagreca,
Natursports, Maksim Shmeljov)

Library of Congress Cataloging-in-Publication Data
Arnold, Quinn M.
Monster trucks / Quinn M. Arnold.
p. cm. — (Seedlings)
Includes bibliographical references and index.
Summary: A kindergarten-level introduction to monster
trucks, covering their purpose, where they are found, the
people who drive them, and such defining features as their
fiberglass bodies and big wheels.
ISBN 978-1-60818-791-1 (hardcover)
ISBN 978-1-62832-387-0 (pbk)
ISBN 978-1-56660-821-3 (eBook)
This title has been submitted for
CIP processing under LCCN 2016937134.

CCSS: RI.K.1, 2, 3, 4, 5, 6, 7;
RI.1.1, 2, 3, 4, 5, 6, 7; RF.K.1, 3; RF.1.1

First Edition HC 9 8 7 6 5 4 3 2 1
First Edition PBK 9 8 7 6 5 4 3 2 1

TABLE OF CONTENTS

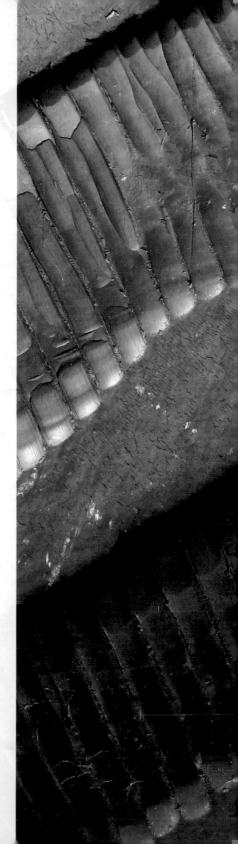

Hello, monster trucks!

Monster trucks are tall trucks. They race on dirt tracks.

They crush other trucks!

A tough monster truck body is made of fiberglass.

The truck's name is painted on the body.

The body sits on the chassis. This part holds the engine. The wheels are below.

Inside the truck is a special chair. A six-part seat belt keeps the driver in the chair.

A monster truck has four big wheels.

They are as tall
as some adults!

Monster trucks
do tricks. They
jump high into
the air!

Their big wheels come crashing down.

17

Goodbye, monster trucks!

Picture a Monster Truck

body

engine

exhaust pipe

chassis

axle

wheels

chassis: the metal frame of a vehicle

fiberglass: a durable material made of plastic and glass

Read More

Gordon, Nick. *Monster Trucks.*
Minneapolis: Bellwether Media, 2014.

Mason, Paul. *Monster Trucks.*
Mankato, Minn.: Amicus, 2011.

Websites

Complete the Picture: Monster Truck Wheels
http://www.activityvillage.co.uk/complete-the-picture
-monster-truck-wheels
Draw and color the body of a monster truck.

Monster Truck Craft
http://www.littlefamilyfun.com/2014/01/monster-truck
-craft.html
Use a toy truck, paint, and paper to make a monster truck.

Index